LOOK AT
SKIN, SHELL
AND SCALE

Franklin Watts
12a Golden Square
London W1R 4AB

Franklin Watts Inc.
387 Park Avenue South
New York
N.Y. 10016

Franklin Watts Australia
14 Mars Road
Lane Cove
N.S.W. 2066

UK ISBN: 0836313 832 2
US ISBN: 0-531-10722-7

Editor: Ruth Thomson
Design: K and Co.
Illustrations: Simon Roulstone
Phototypeset by Lineage Ltd, Watford
Printed in Italy
by G. Canale & C S.p.A. - Turin

Picture credits:
Heather Angel 6, 8, 11, 14a, 15b, 24, 26, 27, 29a, 29b, 29c
Reg Horlock 4, 12
P Morris 15a
Planet Earth 7, 13, 14b, 16, 18, 25, 28
Soames Summerhays 20
Survival Anglia 10, 17, 22
Zefa 19a, 19b, 21

Front cover: ZEFA

LOOK AT
SKIN, SHELL
AND SCALE

Henry Pluckrose

FRANKLIN WATTS
London • New York • Sydney • Toronto

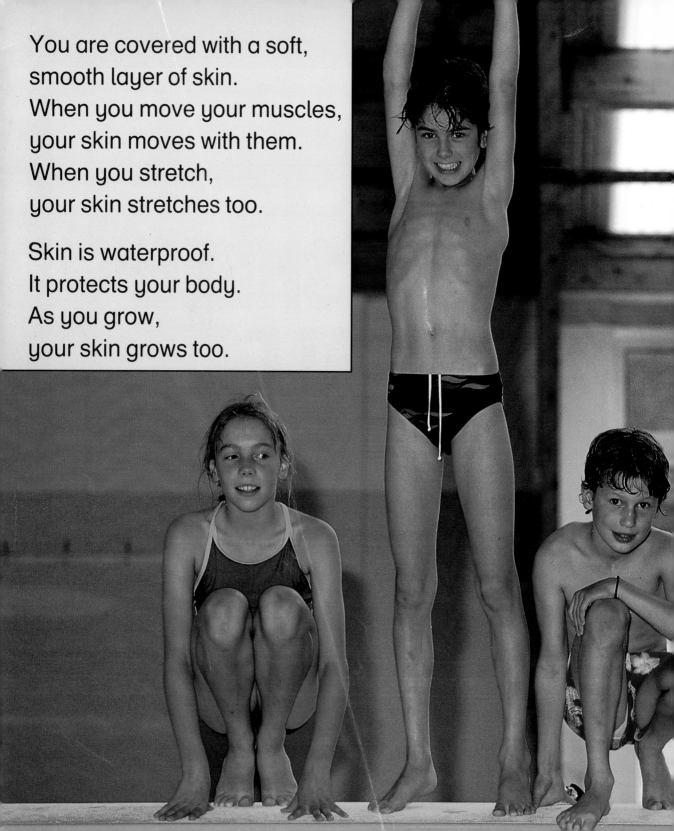

You are covered with a soft,
smooth layer of skin.
When you move your muscles,
your skin moves with them.
When you stretch,
your skin stretches too.

Skin is waterproof.
It protects your body.
As you grow,
your skin grows too.

Not all creatures are covered with skin.
The sea urchin lives inside a hard shell,
made up of tiny plates.
The plates fit together to protect
the sea urchin's soft body.

This rock is covered with limpets.
The limpet grips the rock with the underside
of its body.
Its soft body is protected by its shell.

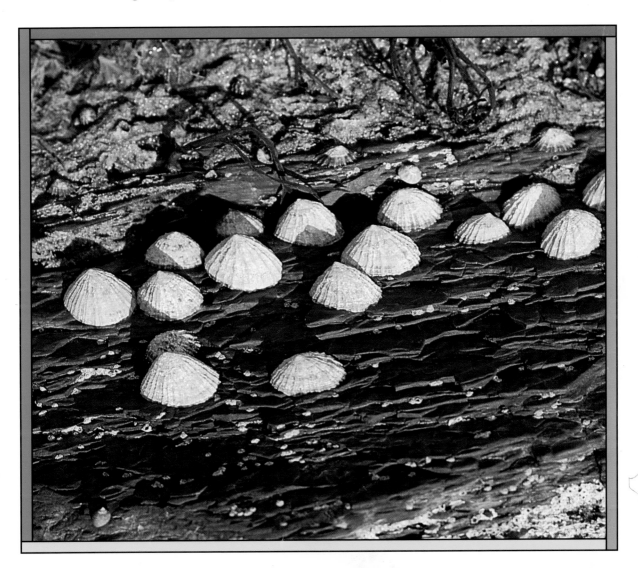

How many different types of shellfish can you see in this rock pool?
Which of them do you think can move most easily?

Creatures with shells also live on land.
The snail lives in a shell,
which is often beautifully patterned.
The shell gets bigger as the body inside it grows.

The slug belongs to the same family
as the snail, but it has no shell.

Squeeze your arm tightly.
Can you feel the bone beneath the skin?

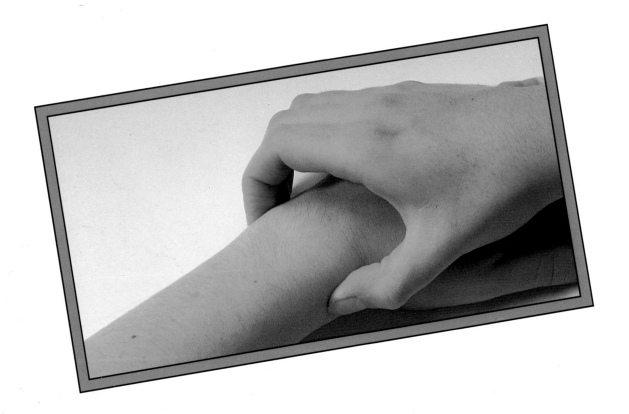

Bones form your skeleton.
The skeleton gives your body its shape.
It protects important organs
and supports your weight.

woodlouse

Some animals have no skeleton.
Their body is protected by a hard covering.
The covering gives the body its shape
and protects its soft flesh.
These creatures are called crustaceans.

Some crustaceans live in the sea.

lobster

crab

shrimp

prawn

15

This is an insect called a stag beetle.
Its soft body is covered with a hard skin
called chitin.

The tortoise has a shell
made of scales of keratin.
(Our fingernails are also made of keratin.)
Bones join its body to its shell.

snake

Snakes, lizards, crocodiles, alligators
and tortoises are reptiles.
All reptiles have scaly skin.

Look at the throat
of this crocodile.
You can see
how the scales
overlap.

On the crocodile's back,
they make a thick shield.

Most reptiles live in hot, dry lands.
However hot the sun is, reptiles never sweat
(lose water) through their scaly skins.
When the scales wear away on this Komodo dragon,
new ones grow to replace them.

A snake does not lose its scales,
it sheds its whole skin.
A new skin grows beneath the old one.

The pangolin is an unusual mammal.
Its body is covered with scales.
When it is frightened, the pangolin rolls up
into a tight ball, and the scales become spikes.

Some creatures like this frog,
live both in water and on land.
They are called amphibians.

Some amphibians have a scaly skin.
Some amphibians have a skin which is rough,
but not scaly.

great crested newt

Amphibians have a special sort of skin.
The skin of this toad can absorb (breathe)
oxygen from the air and from water.

Most fishes have scales.
The scales on fish are tiny plates,
which overlap to cover the whole body.

goldfish

The stickleback has no scales.
Its body is protected with thin layers
of bone.

The colours and patterns on the shells and skins of animals often help protect them from their enemies.
Can you see this fish?

Look at your skin. It is smooth, not scaly.

In how many ways is your skin different from the outer covering of fish, reptiles, amphibians and crustaceans? How is it the same?

tortoise

viper

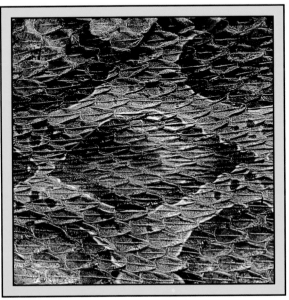

herring

Things to do

● Make a collection of sea shells. Try to identify them.

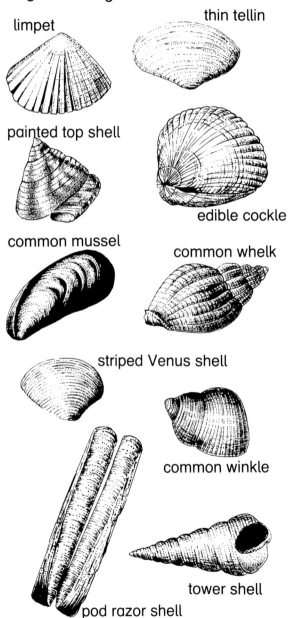

limpet

thin tellin

painted top shell

edible cockle

common mussel

common whelk

striped Venus shell

common winkle

pod razor shell

tower shell

● Make a collage by arranging different shells into patterns or into a picture. Mount the shells on a piece of cardboard with strong, PVA glue.

● Make a shell model by gluing shells together with PVA glue

● When you next visit a zoo or an animal park, make a list of the different animal families you find there. Divide your list into classifications like those below.

ANIMAL FAMILY	
mammal	elephant lion
reptile	lizard snake
crustacean	shrimp crab lobster
insect	ant

Words and sayings

● Can you find out what these words and sayings mean?

Skin

By the skin of one's teeth
Sisters under the skin
He's all skin and bone.
To get under one's skin
To escape with one's skin
To jump out of one's skin
To save one's skin
To keep one's eyes skinned
Do not divide the skin until you have caught the creature.

skin-deep
skin-diver
skinflint
skinful
skin-head
skin-tight
skinner
skinny

Scales

scale armour
scaler
scaly
scale work

To remove the scales from one's eyes

Shells

shellback
shellfish
shell-money
shell-heap
shell-egg
shell-shaped

To shell out
The shell of a boat
To be just a hollow shell
To creep out from one's shell

Can you find out?

'Whose father went hunting to get a rabbit skin?'

Who poured water from the river Nile over his scales to make them shine?

Who put cockle shells in her garden?

Try to make up some more questions like these.

● Make a list of creatures which have no skeleton. These creatures are called invertebrates.

Index